Redesigning Realigning Rediscovering me.

JOURNAL FOR SELF-DISCOVERY

Astrid Ferguson

… this Journal Belongs to:

For the Year of:

Redesigning, Realigning, Rediscovering Me.

Hey Writer!

Welcome to *Redesigning, Realigning, Rediscovering Me*. This journal was crafted as a tool for reconnecting with our inner voice. Consider it a treasure trove of deep secrets of unlocking who you truly are through introspective writing practice.

After migrating to the United States from Dominican Republic, I didn't have many friends and the English language was difficult for me to grasp. Naturally, journals became my friends, companions, therapist, and patient English teachers to practice conversation. Journaling has been a pivotal tool in establishing honest and sincere inner dialogue. They have helped me record thoughts and emotions as I've transitioned and evolved through many challenges in my life. I've had the safety of journal pages to share uncomfortable stories. Having a daily writing practice helped me find strength in my vulnerabilities. That is the gift I hope you uncover in these pages, writer.

Redesigning, Realigning, Rediscovering Me is a 90-day practice organized in morning page prompts, daily highlights, weekly accomplishment tracker, vision-mapping, affirmations, inspiring quotes and much more. The prompts are designed to help you find clarity within your personal story. This journal is intended to be reviewed and held, not closed once the prompts are completed.

So be honest, truthful, and have fun redesigning, realigning, rediscovering yourself. You deserve to reconnect with yourself. You deserve to find the clarity you seek.

Thank you for choosing yourself within the pages of *Redesigning, Realigning, Rediscovering Me*.

Astrid Ferguson

I'M COMMITTING TO...

- **84** morning pages
- **84** daily highlights
- **12** weekly accomplishments
- **6** quotes
- **4** realigning affirmations
- **4** vision mapping exercises
- **4** live checkins
- **3** letter writing exercises
- **2** thought reframing exercises
- **1** poem

 # Morning Pages

DATE / /

WHEN I LOOK IN THE MIRROR I SEE...

WHEN I DRINK MY MORNING COFFEE/TEA/DRINK I FEEL...

THE FIRST THING I WANT TO DO THIS MORNING IS...

Redesigning. Realigning. Rediscovering Me.

Highlights of My Day

DATE / /

Redesigning, Realigning, Rediscovering me

Morning Pages

DATE   /   /

I WOKE UP THINKING...

I FEEL LIKE I'M...

THIS MORNING I WANT TO...

Redesigning. Realigning. Rediscovering Me

Highlights of My Day

DATE / /

Redesigning. Realigning. Rediscovering Me

Morning Pages

DATE   /   /

I FIND MYSELF WANTING...

I AM GRATEFUL TO HAVE...

THIS MORNING I'M CHOOSING...

Redesigning. Realigning. Rediscovering me.

Highlights of My Day

DATE / /

Redesigning. Realigning. Rediscovering me.

 # Morning Pages

DATE / /

I WANT TO FEEL BUT I CAN'T GET OVER...

I KEEP COMPARING MYSELF TO...

I AM PRACTICING SELF-COMPASSION TODAY BY:

Redesigning. Realigning. Rediscovering Me.

Highlights of My Day

DATE / /

Redesigning. Realigning. Rediscovering me.

Morning Pages

DATE / /

I FEEL MY SPIRITUALITY IS...

I WANT TO CONNECT WITH MY SPIRITUALITY BECAUSE...

THIS MORNING I AM CONNECTING WITH MY HIGHER SELF BY:

Redesigning, Realigning, Rediscovering Me

# Highlights of My Day

DATE / /

Redesigning. Realigning. Rediscovering Me

DATE / /

I SEE THE WORLD AROUND ME AND THINK...

I FEEL CONNECTED OR DISCONNECTED TO THOSE AROUND ME BECAUSE...

THIS MORNING I AM CHOOSING TO CONNECT WITH...

Redesigning. Realigning. Rediscovering Me.

Highlights of My Day

DATE   /   /

Redesigning, Realigning, Rediscovering Me.

DATE / /

I WANT TO IMPROVE...

I WANT TO FEEL ____ THROUGHOUT THE DAY BECAUSE...

I AM REAFFIRMING MY NEEDS BY...

Redesigning, Realigning, Rediscovering Me

Highlights of My Day

DATE / /

Redesigning, Realigning, Rediscovering Me

Weekly Accomplishments

DATE / /

m

t

w

t

f

s

WHAT DID I LEARN ABOUT MYSELF THIS WEEK?

Redesigning. Realigning. Rediscovering Me.

STARGAZING AND REALIGNING MY DESIRES

Redesigning. Realigning. Rediscovering Me.

IDENTITY IS A MOVING TARGET, IT NEVER REACHES AN ENDPOINT.

David Eagleman

Morning Pages

DATE / /

WHEN I LOOK IN THE MIRROR I SEE...

WHEN I DRINK MY MORNING COFFEE/TEA/DRINK I FEEL...

THE FIRST THING I WANT TO DO THIS MORNING IS...

Redesigning. Realigning. Rediscovering me

Highlights of My Day

DATE / /

Redesigning. Realigning. Rediscovering Me.

Morning Pages

DATE __ / __ / __

I WOKE UP THINKING...

I FEEL LIKE I'M...

THIS MORNING I WANT TO...

Redesigning. Realigning. Rediscovering Me.

Highlights of My Day

DATE / /

Redesigning. Realigning. Rediscovering Me.

DATE   /   /

I FIND MYSELF WANTING...

I AM GRATEFUL FOR TO HAVE...

THIS MORNING I'M CHOOSING...

Redesigning. Realigning. Rediscovering Me.

Highlights of My Day

DATE / /

Redesigning, Realigning, Rediscovering me

DATE / /

I WANT TO FEEL BUT I CAN'T GET OVER...

I KEEP COMPARING MYSELF TO...

I AM PRACTICING SELF-COMPASSION TODAY BY:

Redesigning. Realigning. Rediscovering Me.

Highlights of My Day

DATE / /

Redesigning, Realigning, Rediscovering Me

DATE / /

I FEEL MY SPIRITUALITY IS...

I WANT TO CONNECT WITH MY SPIRITUALITY BECAUSE...

THIS MORNING I AM CONNECTING WITH MY HIGHER SELF BY:

Redesigning. Realigning. Rediscovering Me.

Highlights of My Day

DATE / /

Redesigning, Realigning, Rediscovering Me

DATE   /   /

I SEE THE WORLD AROUND ME AND THINK...

I FEEL CONNECTED OR DISCONNECTED TO THOSE AROUND ME BECAUSE...

THIS MORNING I AM CHOOSING TO CONNECT WITH...

Redesigning. Realigning. Rediscovering Me.

# Highlights of My Day

DATE / /

Redesigning. Realigning. Rediscovering Me.

Morning Pages

DATE / /

I WANT TO IMPROVE...

I WANT TO FEEL ____ THROUGHOUT THE DAY BECAUSE...

I AM REAFFIRMING MY NEEDS BY...

Redesigning. Realigning. Rediscovering me.

Highlights of My Day

DATE / /

Redesigning. Realigning. Rediscovering Me.

Weekly Accomplishments

DATE / /

(m) (t)

(t)

WHAT DID I LEARN ABOUT MYSELF THIS WEEK?

Redesigning. Realigning. Rediscovering me

How do I feel about my...

Redesigning. Realigning. Rediscovering Me.

5 Grounding Affirmations

01 — I am loving who I'm becoming

02 — I am ready to receive all life has to offer

03 — I am worthy of living a life beyond survival

04 — I love everything about me right now

05 — I am deserving of a joyful, peaceful and prosperous life

DATE   /   /

WHEN I LOOK IN THE MIRROR I SEE...

WHEN I DRINK MY MORNING COFFEE/TEA/DRINK I FEEL...

THE FIRST THING I WANT TO DO THIS MORNING IS...

Redesigning. Realigning. Rediscovering Me.

Highlights of My Day

DATE / /

Redesigning. Realigning. Rediscovering Me.

Morning Pages

DATE / /

I WOKE UP THINKING...

I FEEL LIKE I'M...

THIS MORNING I WANT TO...

Redesigning. Realigning. Rediscovering Me.

# Highlights of My Day

DATE   /   /

Redesigning. Realigning. Rediscovering Me.

DATE   /   /

I FIND MYSELF WANTING...

I AM GRATEFUL TO HAVE...

THIS MORNING I'M CHOOSING...

Redesigning. Realigning. Rediscovering Me.

Highlights of My Day

DATE / /

Redesigning. Realigning. Rediscovering Me.

Morning Pages

DATE / /

I WANT TO FEEL BUT I CAN'T GET OVER...

I KEEP COMPARING MYSELF TO...

I AM PRACTICING SELF-COMPASSION TODAY BY:

Redesigning. Realigning. Rediscovering Me

Highlights of My Day

DATE / /

Redesigning. Realigning. Rediscovering Me.

DATE / /

I FEEL MY SPIRITUALITY IS...

I WANT TO CONNECT WITH MY SPIRITUALITY BECAUSE...

THIS MORNING I AM CONNECTING WITH MY HIGHER SELF BY:

Redesigning. Realigning. Rediscovering Me.

Highlights of My Day

DATE / /

Redesigning, Realigning, Rediscovering Me

DATE   /   /

I SEE THE WORLD AROUND ME AND THINK...

I FEEL CONNECTED OR DISCONNECTED TO THOSE AROUND ME BECAUSE...

THIS MORNING I AM CHOOSING TO CONNECT WITH...

Redesigning, Realigning, Rediscovering Me

Highlights of My Day

DATE / /

Redesigning, Realigning, Rediscovering Me.

DATE   /   /

I WANT TO IMPROVE...

I WANT TO FEEL ____ THROUGHOUT THE DAY BECAUSE...

I AM REAFFIRMING MY NEEDS BY...

Redesigning. Realigning. Rediscovering Me.

Highlights of My Day

DATE / /

Redesigning. Realigning. Rediscovering me.

Weekly Accomplishments

DATE / /

M

T

W

T

F

S

WHAT DID I LEARN ABOUT MYSELF THIS WEEK?

Redesigning, Realigning, Rediscovering Me

STARGAZING AND REALIGNING MY DESIRES

Redesigning. Realigning. Rediscovering Me

NEVER ABANDON YOUR DREAMS BECAUSE SOMEONE LIVING THEIR NIGHTMARE TOLD YOU SO.

Astrid Ferguson

Morning Pages

DATE   /   /

WHEN I LOOK IN THE MIRROR I SEE...

WHEN I DRINK MY MORNING COFFEE/TEA/DRINK I FEEL...

THE FIRST THING I WANT TO DO THIS MORNING IS...

Redesigning. Realigning. Rediscovering Me.

Highlights of My Day

DATE / /

Redesigning. Realigning. Rediscovering Me.

DATE / /

I WOKE UP THINKING...

I FEEL LIKE I'M...

THIS MORNING I WILL...

Redesigning. Realigning. Rediscovering Me.

Highlights of My Day

DATE / /

Redesigning. Realigning. Rediscovering Me.

DATE / /

I FIND MYSELF WANTING...

I AM GRATEFUL TO HAVE...

THIS MORNING I'M CHOOSING...

Redesigning. Realigning. Rediscovering Me.

Highlights of My Day

DATE / /

Redesigning, Realigning, Rediscovering Me.

DATE   /   /

I WANT TO FEEL BUT I CAN'T GET OVER...

I KEEP COMPARING MYSELF TO...

I AM PRACTICING SELF-COMPASSION TODAY BY:

Redesigning. Realigning. Rediscovering Me

Highlights of My Day

DATE   /   /

Redesigning. Realigning. Rediscovering Me.

Morning Pages

DATE   /   /

I FEEL MY SPIRITUALITY IS...

I WANT TO CONNECT WITH MY SPIRITUALITY BECAUSE...

THIS MORNING I AM CONNECTING WITH MY HIGHER SELF BY:

Redesigning. Realigning. Rediscovering Me.

Highlights of My Day

DATE / /

Redesigning. Realigning. Rediscovering Me.

DATE   /   /

I SEE THE WORLD AROUND ME AND THINK...

I FEEL CONNECTED OR DISCONNECTED TO THOSE AROUND ME BECAUSE...

THIS MORNING I AM CHOOSING TO CONNECT WITH...

Redesigning. Realigning. Rediscovering me.

Highlights of My Day

DATE / /

Redesigning, Realigning, Rediscovering Me

DATE   /   /

I WANT TO IMPROVE...

I WANT TO FEEL ____ THROUGHOUT THE DAY BECAUSE...

I AM REAFFIRMING MY NEEDS BY...

Redesigning. Realigning. Rediscovering me.

Highlights of My Day

DATE / /

Redesigning, Realigning, Rediscovering me.

Weekly Accomplishments

DATE / /

(m)　　　(t)　　　(w)

(t)　　　(f)　　　(s)

WHAT DID I LEARN ABOUT MYSELF THIS WEEK?

Redesigning. Realigning. Rediscovering me.

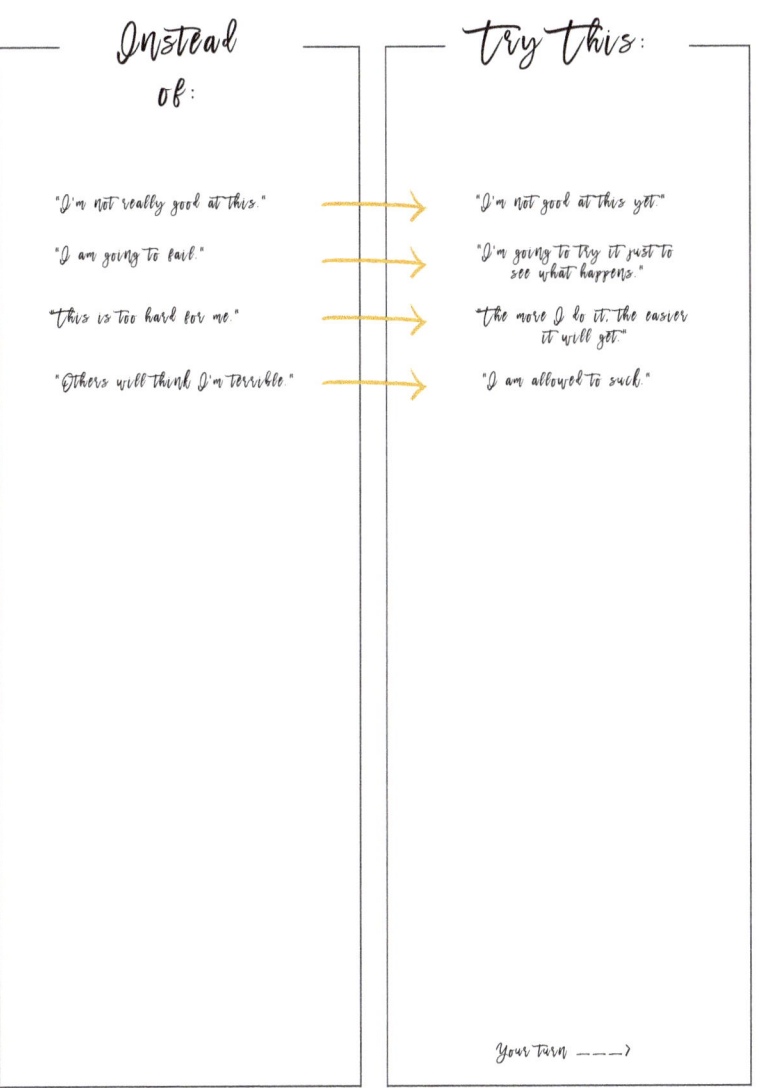

Instead of:	Try this:
"I'm not really good at this."	"I'm not good at this yet."
"I am going to fail."	"I'm going to try it just to see what happens."
"This is too hard for me."	"The more I do it, the easier it will get."
"Others will think I'm terrible."	"I am allowed to suck."

Your turn ----»

Redesigning. Realigning. Rediscovering me.

Instead of:	Try this:

Redesigning. Realigning. Rediscovering me.

COURAGE DOESN'T ALWAYS ROAR. SOMETIMES COURAGE IS THE QUIET VOICE AT THE END OF THE DAY SAYING, "I WILL TRY AGAIN TOMORROW."

Mary Anne Radmacher

DATE   /   /

WHEN I LOOK IN THE MIRROR I SEE...

WHEN I DRINK MY MORNING COFFEE/TEA/DRINK I FEEL...

THE FIRST THING I WANT TO DO THIS MORNING IS...

Redesigning. Realigning. Rediscovering Me.

Highlights of My Day

DATE   /   /

Redesigning, Realigning, Rediscovering Me.

DATE / /

I WOKE UP THINKING...

I FEEL LIKE I'M...

THIS MORNING I WILL...

Redesigning. Realigning. Rediscovering me.

Highlights of My Day

DATE / /

Redesigning. Realigning. Rediscovering Me.

Morning Pages

DATE / /

I FIND MYSELF WANTING...

I AM GRATEFUL TO HAVE...

THIS MORNING I'M CHOOSING...

Redesigning. Realigning. Rediscovering me.

Highlights of My Day

DATE / /

Redesigning. Realigning. Rediscovering Me.

DATE   /   /

I WANT TO FEEL BUT I CAN'T GET OVER...

I KEEP COMPARING MYSELF TO...

I AM PRACTICING SELF-COMPASSION TODAY BY:

Redesigning. Realigning. Rediscovering me.

Highlights of My Day

DATE   /   /

Redesigning. Realigning. Rediscovering Me.

DATE   /   /

I FEEL MY SPIRITUALITY IS...

I WANT TO CONNECT WITH MY SPIRITUALITY BECAUSE...

THIS MORNING I AM CONNECTING WITH MY HIGHER SELF BY:

Redesigning. Realigning. Rediscovering me.

Highlights of My Day

DATE / /

Redesigning, Realigning, Rediscovering Me.

Morning Pages

DATE / /

I SEE THE WORLD AROUND ME AND THINK...

I FEEL CONNECTED OR DISCONNECTED TO THOSE AROUND ME BECAUSE...

THIS MORNING I AM CHOOSING TO CONNECT WITH...

Redesigning. Realigning. Rediscovering Me.

Highlights of My Day

DATE   /   /

Redesigning, Realigning, Rediscovering me.

DATE   /   /

I WANT TO IMPROVE...

I WANT TO FEEL ____ THROUGHOUT THE DAY BECAUSE...

I AM REAFFIRMING MY NEEDS BY...

Redesigning. Realigning. Rediscovering me

Highlights of My Day

DATE   /   /

Redesigning, Realigning, Rediscovering Me

Weekly Accomplishments

DATE / /

m t w

t f s

WHAT DID I LEARN ABOUT MYSELF THIS WEEK?

Redesigning. Realigning. Rediscovering Me.

How do I want to feel about my...

Environment

Health

Family

Finances

Relationships

Spirituality

Redesigning, Realigning, Rediscovering me.

5
Positive Money Affirmations

01 — I am where the money resides

02 — Money will flow abundantly to me

03 — Money is energy and I am open to receiving it

04 — I am deserving and worthy of living a wealthy bad ass life

05 — Money is my favorite tool of choice for building the life I want and deserve

Morning Pages

DATE / /

WHEN I LOOK IN THE MIRROR I SEE...

WHEN I DRINK MY MORNING COFFEE/TEA/DRINK I FEEL...

THE FIRST THING I WANT TO DO THIS MORNING IS...

Redesigning. Realigning. Rediscovering Me.

Highlights of My Day

DATE / /

Redesigning, Realigning, Rediscovering Me.

 # Morning Pages

DATE   /   /

I WOKE UP THINKING...

I FEEL LIKE I'M...

THIS MORNING I WANT TO...

Redesigning. Realigning. Rediscovering me.

Highlights of My Day

DATE / /

Redesigning. Realigning. Rediscovering Me.

DATE / /

I FIND MYSELF WANTING...

I AM GRATEFUL TO HAVE...

THIS MORNING I'M CHOOSING...

Redesigning. Realigning. Rediscovering me.

Highlights of My Day

DATE / /

Redesigning. Realigning. Rediscovering me.

DATE   /   /

I WANT TO FEEL BUT I CAN'T GET OVER...

I KEEP COMPARING MYSELF TO...

I AM PRACTICING SELF-COMPASSION TODAY BY:

Redesigning, Realigning, Rediscovering Me

Highlights of My Day

DATE / /

Redesigning, Realigning, Rediscovering Me.

Morning Pages

DATE / /

I FEEL MY SPIRITUALITY IS...

I WANT TO CONNECT WITH MY SPIRITUALITY BECAUSE...

THIS MORNING I AM CONNECTING WITH MY HIGHER SELF BY:

Redesigning. Realigning. Rediscovering me.

Highlights of My Day

DATE   /   /

Redesigning. Realigning. Rediscovering me.

Morning Pages

DATE / /

I SEE THE WORLD AROUND ME AND THINK...

I FEEL CONNECTED OR DISCONNECTED TO THOSE AROUND ME BECAUSE...

THIS MORNING I AM CHOOSING TO CONNECT WITH...

Redesigning. Realigning. Rediscovering Me.

Highlights of My Day

DATE / /

Redesigning, Realigning, Rediscovering Me

DATE   /   /

I WANT TO IMPROVE...

I WANT TO FEEL ____ THROUGHOUT THE DAY BECAUSE...

I AM REAFFIRMING MY NEEDS BY...

Redesigning, Realigning, Rediscovering Me.

Highlights of My Day

DATE   /   /

Redesigning. Realigning. Rediscovering me.

Weekly Accomplishments

DATE / /

- m
- t
- w
- t
- f
- s

WHAT DID I LEARN ABOUT MYSELF THIS WEEK?

Redesigning. Realigning. Rediscovering Me

Letter to my inner child

DATE / /

Redesigning. Realigning. Rediscovering me.

IT IS BETTER TO BE HATED FOR WHAT YOU ARE THEN TO BE LOVED FOR WHAT YOU ARE NOT.

André Gide

DATE / /

WHEN I LOOK IN THE MIRROR I SEE...

WHEN I DRINK MY MORNING COFFEE/TEA/DRINK I FEEL...

THE FIRST THING I WANT TO DO THIS MORNING IS...

Redesigning. Realigning. Rediscovering me.

Highlights of My Day

DATE / /

Redesigning, Realigning, Rediscovering Me.

DATE / /

I WOKE UP THINKING...

I FEEL LIKE I'M...

THIS MORNING I WANT TO...

Redesigning. Realigning. Rediscovering Me

Highlights of My Day

DATE / /

Redesigning. Realigning. Rediscovering Me

DATE / /

I FIND MYSELF WANTING...

I AM GRATEFUL FOR TO HAVE...

THIS MORNING I'M CHOOSING...

Redesigning. Realigning. Rediscovering me.

Highlights of My Day

DATE / /

Redesigning. Realigning. Rediscovering Me.

Morning Pages

DATE / /

I WANT TO FEEL BUT I CAN'T GET OVER...

I KEEP COMPARING MYSELF TO...

I AM PRACTICING SELF-COMPASSION TODAY BY:

Redesigning, Realigning, Rediscovering Me

Highlights of My Day

DATE   /   /

Redesigning. Realigning. Rediscovering Me

DATE / /

I FEEL MY SPIRITUALITY IS...

I WANT TO CONNECT WITH MY SPIRITUALITY BECAUSE...

THIS MORNING I AM CONNECTING WITH MY HIGHER SELF BY:

Redesigning. Realigning. Rediscovering Me

Highlights of My Day

DATE   /   /

Redesigning. Realigning. Rediscovering Me.

DATE / /

I SEE THE WORLD AROUND ME AND THINK...

I FEEL CONNECTED OR DISCONNECTED TO THOSE AROUND ME BECAUSE...

THIS MORNING I AM CHOOSING TO CONNECT WITH...

Redesigning. Realigning. Rediscovering Me.

Highlights of My Day

DATE / /

Redesigning. Realigning. Rediscovering Me.

DATE / /

I WANT TO IMPROVE...

I WANT TO FEEL ____ THROUGHOUT THE DAY BECAUSE...

I AM REAFFIRMING MY NEEDS BY...

Redesigning. Realigning. Rediscovering me.

Highlights of My Day

DATE / /

Redesigning. Realigning. Rediscovering Me.

Weekly Accomplishments

DATE / /

(m) (t) (w)

(t) (f) (s)

WHAT DID I LEARN ABOUT MYSELF THIS WEEK?

STARGAZING AND REALIGNING MY DESIRES

Redesigning, Realigning, Rediscovering Me

5
Mindset Affirmations

FILL IN THE BLANK ↙

01   I love my ability to (   ).

02   I give myself permission to walk away from people, relationships and spaces that no longer serve me.

03   I trust and value myself more than anyones opinion.

04   My past failures does not make me a failure; I am a work in progress because of them.

05   I am who I decide I am, not what my thoughts tell me I am.

DATE / /

WHEN I LOOK IN THE MIRROR I SEE...

WHEN I DRINK MY MORNING COFFEE/TEA/DRINK I FEEL...

THE FIRST THING I WANT TO DO THIS MORNING IS...

Redesigning. Realigning. Rediscovering Me.

Highlights of My Day

DATE   /   /

Redesigning. Realigning. Rediscovering Me.

DATE   /   /

I WOKE UP THINKING...

I FEEL LIKE I'M...

THIS MORNING I WANT TO...

Redesigning. Realigning. Rediscovering Me.

Highlights of My Day

DATE / /

Redesigning, Realigning, Rediscovering Me

DATE / /

I FIND MYSELF WANTING...

I AM GRATEFUL TO HAVE...

THIS MORNING I'M CHOOSING...

Redesigning. Realigning. Rediscovering me

Highlights of My Day

DATE / /

Redesigning. Realigning. Rediscovering me.

DATE / /

I WANT TO FEEL BUT I CAN'T GET OVER...

I KEEP COMPARING MYSELF TO...

I AM PRACTICING SELF-COMPASSION TODAY BY:

Redesigning. Realigning. Rediscovering Me.

Highlights of My Day

DATE   /   /

Redesigning. Realigning. Rediscovering Me.

Morning Pages

DATE / /

I FEEL MY SPIRITUALITY IS...

I WANT TO CONNECT WITH MY SPIRITUALITY BECAUSE...

THIS MORNING I AM CONNECTING WITH MY HIGHER SELF BY:

Redesigning. Realigning. Rediscovering Me.

Highlights of My Day

DATE / /

Redesigning. Realigning. Rediscovering me.

DATE   /   /

I SEE THE WORLD AROUND ME AND THINK...

I FEEL CONNECTED OR DISCONNECTED TO THOSE AROUND ME BECAUSE...

THIS MORNING I AM CHOOSING TO CONNECT WITH...

Redesigning. Realigning. Rediscovering me.

Highlights of My Day

DATE / /

Redesigning. Realigning. Rediscovering me.

DATE   /   /

I WANT TO IMPROVE...

I WANT TO FEEL _ _ _ _ THROUGHOUT THE DAY BECAUSE...

I AM REAFFIRMING MY NEEDS BY...

Redesigning. Realigning. Rediscovering Me.

Highlights of My Day

DATE / /

Redesigning. Realigning. Rediscovering Me.

Weekly Accomplishments

DATE   /   /

m   **t**   **w**

t   **f**   **s**

WHAT DID I LEARN ABOUT MYSELF THIS WEEK?

Redesigning. Realigning. Rediscovering Me.

STARGAZING AND REALIGNING MY DESIRES

Redesigning, Realigning, Rediscovering me.

FORGIVENESS MEANS GIVING UP ALL HOPE FOR A BETTER PAST.

Note to self:
I forgive myself for everything I wish I had done.

Today, I surrender the wish to have done better.

Lily Tomlin

DATE / /

WHEN I LOOK IN THE MIRROR I SEE...

WHEN I DRINK MY MORNING COFFEE/TEA/DRINK I FEEL...

THE FIRST THING I WANT TO DO THIS MORNING IS...

Redesigning. Realigning. Rediscovering me.

Highlights of My Day

DATE / /

Redesigning. Realigning. Rediscovering Me.

DATE / /

I WOKE UP THINKING...

I FEEL LIKE I'M...

THIS MORNING I WANT TO...

Redesigning. Realigning. Rediscovering Me.

Highlights of My Day

DATE / /

Redesigning, Realigning, Rediscovering Me

Morning Pages

DATE / /

I FIND MYSELF WANTING...

I AM GRATEFUL TO HAVE...

THIS MORNING I'M CHOOSING...

Redesigning. Realigning. Rediscovering Me.

Highlights of My Day

DATE / /

Redesigning. Realigning. Rediscovering Me.

DATE / /

I WANT TO FEEL BUT I CAN'T GET OVER...

I KEEP COMPARING MYSELF TO...

I AM PRACTICING SELF-COMPASSION TODAY BY:

Redesigning. Realigning. Rediscovering me.

Highlights of My Day

DATE   /   /

Redesigning. Realigning. Rediscovering Me.

DATE / /

I FEEL MY SPIRITUALITY IS...

I WANT TO CONNECT WITH MY SPIRITUALITY BECAUSE...

THIS MORNING I AM CONNECTING WITH MY HIGHER SELF BY:

Redesigning. Realigning. Rediscovering Me.

Highlights of My Day

DATE   /   /

Redesigning, Realigning, Rediscovering Me.

DATE / /

I SEE THE WORLD AROUND ME AND THINK...

I FEEL CONNECTED OR DISCONNECTED TO THOSE AROUND ME BECAUSE...

THIS MORNING I AM CHOOSING TO CONNECT WITH...

Redesigning. Realigning. Rediscovering me

Highlights of My Day

DATE   /   /

Redesigning. Realigning. Rediscovering Me.

DATE / /

I WANT TO IMPROVE...

I WANT TO FEEL ____ THROUGHOUT THE DAY BECAUSE...

I AM REAFFIRMING MY NEEDS BY...

Redesigning. Realigning. Rediscovering Me.

Highlights of My Day

DATE   /   /

Redesigning. Realigning. Rediscovering Me.

Weekly Accomplishments

DATE / /

(m) (t) (w)

(t) (f) (s)

WHAT DID I LEARN ABOUT MYSELF THIS WEEK?

Redesigning, Realigning, Rediscovering Me.

Letter to future me

DATE / /

Redesigning. Realigning. Rediscovering me.

ONCE YOU BEGIN TO UNDERSTAND WHO YOU REALLY ARE WITHOUT TRYING TO CHANGE, PURPOSE GREETS YOU AT THE ARRIVAL OF YOUR TRANSITIONAL JOURNEY.

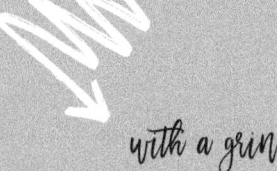

with a grin.

Astrid Ferguson

DATE   /   /

WHEN I LOOK IN THE MIRROR I SEE...

WHEN I DRINK MY MORNING COFFEE/TEA/DRINK I FEEL...

THE FIRST THING I WANT TO DO THIS MORNING IS...

Redesigning, Realigning, Rediscovering Me

Highlights of My Day

DATE / /

Redesigning. Realigning. Rediscovering Me.

Morning Pages

DATE   /   /

I WOKE UP THINKING...

I FEEL LIKE I'M...

THIS MORNING I WANT TO...

Redesigning. Realigning. Rediscovering Me.

Highlights of My Day

DATE   /   /

Redesigning. Realigning. Rediscovering Me.

DATE / /

I FIND MYSELF WANTING...

I AM GRATEFUL TO HAVE...

THIS MORNING I'M CHOOSING...

Redesigning. Realigning. Rediscovering Me.

Highlights of My Day

DATE / /

Redesigning. Realigning. Rediscovering Me.

DATE   /   /

I WANT TO FEEL BUT I CAN'T GET OVER...

I KEEP COMPARING MYSELF TO...

I AM PRACTICING SELF-COMPASSION TODAY BY:

Redesigning. Realigning. Rediscovering Me

Highlights of My Day

DATE / /

Redesigning. Realigning. Rediscovering Me.

Morning Pages

DATE / /

I FEEL MY SPIRITUALITY IS...

I WANT TO CONNECT WITH MY SPIRITUALITY BECAUSE...

THIS MORNING I AM CONNECTING WITH MY HIGHER SELF BY:

Redesigning. Realigning. Rediscovering Me.

Highlights of My Day

DATE   /   /

Redesigning, Realigning, Rediscovering Me

DATE / /

I SEE THE WORLD AROUND ME AND THINK...

I FEEL CONNECTED OR DISCONNECTED TO THOSE AROUND ME BECAUSE...

THIS MORNING I AM CHOOSING TO CONNECT WITH...

Redesigning. Realigning. Rediscovering me.

Highlights of My Day

DATE / /

Redesigning, Realigning, Rediscovering Me

Morning Pages

DATE   /   /

I WANT TO IMPROVE...

I WANT TO FEEL ____ THROUGHOUT THE DAY BECAUSE...

I AM REAFFIRMING MY NEEDS BY...

Redesigning, Realigning, Rediscovering Me

Highlights of My Day

DATE / /

Redesigning, Realigning, Rediscovering Me.

Weekly Accomplishments

DATE / /

- m
- t
- w
- t
- f
- s

WHAT DID I LEARN ABOUT MYSELF THIS WEEK?

Redesigning, Realigning, Rediscovering Me

I am capable List

- [ ]
- [ ]
- [ ]
- [ ]
- [ ]
- [ ]
- [ ]
- [ ]
- [ ]
- [ ]
- [ ]
- [ ]
- [ ]
- [ ]
- [ ]
- [ ]
- [ ]
- [ ]
- [ ]
- [ ]
- [ ]
- [ ]
- [ ]
- [ ]
- [ ]
- [ ]
- [ ]
- [ ]
- [ ]
- [ ]

Redesigning. Realigning. Rediscovering Me.

My Top 5
Realigning Affirmations

01 _____

02 _____

03 _____

04 _____

05 _____

Morning Pages

DATE / /

WHEN I LOOK IN THE MIRROR I SEE...

WHEN I DRINK MY MORNING COFFEE/TEA/DRINK I FEEL...

THE FIRST THING I WANT TO DO THIS MORNING IS...

Redesigning. Realigning. Rediscovering Me.

Highlights of My Day

DATE   /   /

Redesigning, Realigning, Rediscovering Me

DATE / /

I WOKE UP THINKING...

I FEEL LIKE I'M...

THIS MORNING I WANT TO...

Redesigning. Realigning. Rediscovering Me.

Highlights of My Day

DATE / /

Redesigning. Realigning. Rediscovering Me.

Morning Pages

DATE / /

I FIND MYSELF WANTING...

I AM GRATEFUL TO HAVE...

THIS MORNING I'M CHOOSING...

Redesigning. Realigning. Rediscovering Me.

Highlights of My Day

DATE / /

Redesigning. Realigning. Rediscovering Me.

Morning Pages

DATE / /

I WANT TO FEEL BUT I CAN'T GET OVER...

I KEEP COMPARING MYSELF TO...

I AM PRACTICING SELF-COMPASSION TODAY BY:

Redesigning. Realigning. Rediscovering me.

Highlights of My Day

DATE   /   /

Redesigning, Realigning, Rediscovering Me.

Morning Pages

DATE / /

I FEEL MY SPIRITUALITY IS...

I WANT TO CONNECT WITH MY SPIRITUALITY BECAUSE...

THIS MORNING I AM CONNECTING WITH MY HIGHER SELF BY:

Redesigning. Realigning. Rediscovering Me.

Highlights of My Day

DATE / /

Redesigning. Realigning. Rediscovering Me.

Morning Pages

DATE / /

I SEE THE WORLD AROUND ME AND THINK...

I FEEL CONNECTED OR DISCONNECTED TO THOSE AROUND ME BECAUSE...

THIS MORNING I AM CHOOSING TO CONNECT WITH...

Redesigning. Realigning. Rediscovering me.

Highlights of My Day

DATE   /   /

Redesigning, Realigning, Rediscovering Me.

# Morning Pages

DATE / /

I WANT TO IMPROVE...

I WANT TO FEEL ____ THROUGHOUT THE DAY BECAUSE...

I AM REAFFIRMING MY NEEDS BY...

Redesigning. Realigning. Rediscovering Me.

Highlights of My Day

DATE   /   /

Redesigning. Realigning. Rediscovering Me.

Weekly Accomplishments

DATE / /

  w

  s

WHAT DID I LEARN ABOUT MYSELF THIS WEEK?

Redesigning. Realigning. Rediscovering Me.

Letter of encouragement

DATE / /

Redesigning. Realigning. Rediscovering Me.

IF YOU'RE ALWAYS TRYING TO BE NORMAL YOU WILL NEVER KNOW HOW AMAZING YOU CAN BE.

Maya Angelou

DATE   /   /

WHEN I LOOK IN THE MIRROR I SEE...

WHEN I DRINK MY MORNING COFFEE/TEA/DRINK I FEEL...

THE FIRST THING I WANT TO DO THIS MORNING IS...

Redesigning. Realigning. Rediscovering Me.

Highlights of My Day

DATE   /   /

Redesigning. Realigning. Rediscovering Me.

DATE / /

I WOKE UP THINKING...

I FEEL LIKE I'M...

THIS MORNING I WANT TO...

Redesigning, Realigning, Rediscovering Me.

Highlights of My Day

DATE / /

Redesigning. Realigning. Rediscovering Me

DATE / /

I FIND MYSELF WANTING...

I AM GRATEFUL FOR TO HAVE...

THIS MORNING I'M CHOOSING...

Redesigning. Realigning. Rediscovering Me.

Highlights of My Day

DATE / /

Redesigning. Realigning. Rediscovering me

DATE   /   /

I WANT TO FEEL BUT I CAN'T GET OVER...

I KEEP COMPARING MYSELF TO...

I AM PRACTICING SELF-COMPASSION TODAY BY:

Redesigning. Realigning. Rediscovering Me.

Highlights of My Day

DATE   /   /

Redesigning. Realigning. Rediscovering Me.

DATE / /

I FEEL MY SPIRITUALITY IS...

I WANT TO CONNECT WITH MY SPIRITUALITY BECAUSE...

THIS MORNING I AM CONNECTING WITH MY HIGHER SELF BY:

Redesigning. Realigning. Rediscovering Me.

Highlights of My Day

DATE / /

Redesigning. Realigning. Rediscovering Me.

Morning Pages

DATE / /

I SEE THE WORLD AROUND ME AND THINK...

I FEEL CONNECTED OR DISCONNECTED TO THOSE AROUND ME BECAUSE...

THIS MORNING I AM CHOOSING TO CONNECT WITH...

Redesigning, Realigning, Rediscovering Me

Highlights of My Day

DATE / /

Redesigning. Realigning. Rediscovering Me.

Morning Pages

DATE / /

I WANT TO IMPROVE...

I WANT TO FEEL ____ THROUGHOUT THE DAY BECAUSE...

I AM REAFFIRMING MY NEEDS BY...

Redesigning. Realigning. Rediscovering me.

Highlights of My Day

DATE / /

Redesigning. Realigning. Rediscovering Me.

Weekly Accomplishments

DATE / /

(m)   (t)   (w)

(t)   (f)   (s)

WHAT DID I LEARN ABOUT MYSELF THIS WEEK?

Redesigning. Realigning. Rediscovering Me.

My Johari Mirror...

Arena - what I and others know about me	Blindspot - what others know about me but I don't

Facade - what I know about me but others don't	Unknown - what I and others don't know about me

Redesigning, Realigning, Rediscovering me

Redesigning, Realigning, Rediscovering Thy Self

MAYBE YOU ARE EQUAL PARTS MILK AND BUTTER.
MAYBE YOU ARE EQUAL PARTS SALT AND HONEY.

WHICHEVER PARTS MAKE YOU,
YOU WERE CREATED,
CONSTRUCTED,
DERIVED FROM SOMETHING ORIGINAL.

MAYBE YOU PRETENDED TO BE BOTH THE POTTER
AND THE CLAY
SO YOU TRIED TO REDESIGN WHAT FELT RUINED.

MAYBE YOU FELT COMPLETE
UNTIL YOU REDISCOVERED, COMPLETION REMAINS
FOREVER UNFINISHED.

WHATEVER YOU CHOOSE TO FIND IN THE
REDESIGNING
REALIGING
REDISCOVERING THY SELF

ALWAYS REMEMBER, THE STEM IS FRAGILE
BENDING FORWARD WITHOUT ANY INTENTION TO
BREAK.

Astrid Ferguson

Thank You...

So much for completing this daily writing practice. Celebrate yourself for committing to your self-care. I hope you continue this journey by inventing new ways to give back to your wellbeing and develop a new understanding of self.

Joy is found in the small moments of everyday. We may never truly know everything about life or even ourselves, but we can always give ourselves permission to continue redesigning, realigning, and rediscovering ourselves.

Contact Information

Website: www.astridferguson.com
Email: info@astridferguson.com
Instagram: @astrid_ferg
Let's chat!

If we haven't met before, I am a certified professional coach, energy leadership index-master practitioner, author and co-host on Call Your Sister Podcast. My dynamic coaching helps people navigate through unclear transitions by abolishing internal blocks keeping them from creating the work/life balance they desire. So they can ultimately, get back to having fun being authentically themselves. My greatest passion is witnessing people becoming joyful after choosing to let go of everything that no longer serves them and rediscovering who they truly are. So if this is our first *hola (hello)*, I'm delighted to meet you.

Hasta Luego (Farewell)!

www.ingramcontent.com/pod-product-compliance
Lightning Source LLC
Chambersburg PA
CBHW042114100526
44587CB00025B/4049